Love of the Faith

Favorite New Testament Texts

Onesimus Bible Study Series

Chapters by Alumni of Heritage Christian University

Edited by
Bill Bagents

CYPRESS

Love of the Faith: Favorite New Testament Texts

Published by Cypress Publications

Copyright © 2023 by Bill Bagents

Manufactured in the United States of America

Cataloging-in-Publication Data

Love of the faith: favorite New Testament texts/ edited by Bill Bagents

p. cm.

Includes scripture index.

ISBN 978-1-956811-47-6 (pbk.) 978-1-956811-48-3 (ebook)

1. Bible. New Testament—Study and teaching. 2. Christian life—Study and teaching I. Bagents, William Ronald, 1956–, editor. II. Title.

2225.007—dc20

Library of Congress Control Number: 2023942595

Cover design by Brad McKinnon and Brittany Vander Maas.

For information:

Cypress Publications

3625 Helton Drive, PO Box HCU, Florence, AL 35630

www.hcu.edu

Onesimus Bible Study Series

The Onesimus Bible Study Series offers biblical lessons for personal or group study from alumni of International Bible College / Heritage Christian University. Each lesson flows from confidence in Scripture as God's inspired, living, and powerful word. Each respects the ongoing relevance of the Bible as it shows us God's heart and guides our service in the name of Jesus. Every lesson is designed to build faith and encourage Christian living.

Why the name Onesimus? We love the brief book of Philemon, in which Onesimus shines as a stunning example of trusting God more than self or circumstance. The runaway slave met the apostle Paul and encountered God's truth. Out of respect for God — and with Paul's blessing and support — Onesimus chose to return to his owner. He did right by obeying the unfortunate and challenging law of the day despite potentially heavy costs and consequences.

Many of our alumni write beautifully. They also exhibit the servant's heart modeled by Onesimus. Their loyalty to God and submission to Scripture model the faithful excellence of Onesimus. We're blessed to know and serve with such fine brethren. We believe they will bless you too.

Editors of Heritage Christian University Press

Contents

Bible Abbreviations

Old Testament

Gen	Genesis
Exod	Exodus
Lev	Leviticus
Num	Numbers
Deut	Deuteronomy
Josh	Joshua
Judg	Judges
Ruth	Ruth
1–2 Sam	1–2 Samuel
1–2 Kgs	1–2 Kings
1–2 Chr	1–2 Chronicles
Ezra	Ezra
Neh	Nehemiah
Esth	Esther
Job	Job
Ps	Psalms
Prov	Proverbs
Eccl	Ecclesiastes

Song	Song of Solomon
Isa	Isaiah
Jer	Jeremiah
Lam	Lamentations
Ezek	Ezekiel
Dan	Daniel
Hos	Hosea
Joel	Joel
Amos	Amos
Obad	Obadiah
Jonah	Jonah
Mic	Micah
Nah	Nahum
Hab	Habakkuk
Zeph	Zephaniah
Hag	Haggai
Zech	Zechariah
Mal	Malachi

New Testament

Matt	Matthew
Mark	Mark
Luke	Luke
John	John
Acts	Acts
Rom	Romans
1–2 Cor	1–2 Corinthians
Gal	Galatians
Eph	Ephesians
Phil	Philippians
Col	Colossians
1–2 Thess	1–2 Thessalonians
1–2 Tim	1–2 Timothy
Titus	Titus
Phlm	Philemon
Heb	Hebrews
Jas	James
1–2 Pet	1–2 Peter
1–2–3 John	1–2–3 John
Jude	Jude
Rev	Revelation

Love of the Faith

The God of Restoration

Luke 15:11–24

Mike Baker

Focus Passage

Luke 15:11–24

One Main Thing

God is more interested in our restoration than our punishment. We should never be fearful of admitting our wrongs and returning to God. He is patiently looking for our return.

Introduction

Luke 15 is one of the great chapters of the Bible. While surrounded by an audience of those seeking truth as well as those actively criticizing Him, Jesus provides us with three parables pointing to the joy of finding and restoring what has been lost.

In the first, a sheep became separated from the herd

and was rescued by a shepherd. He left others in a safe place to rescue the lost one.

In the second, a coin is somehow misplaced by a woman. The coin, possibly part of an ornamental headband or an important collection, is found only by a diligent search by the woman.

In the third, a son rebels against his father and plots his own course. Upon hitting rock bottom, he realizes his mistakes and determines to rejoin his father.

While all three are similar in that something is lost, they differ in the ways in which the subject is lost and restored. The shepherd takes responsibility and goes out to find the missing sheep, who had wandered away aimlessly. He finds the sheep, places it on his shoulders, and transports it back to the others. He shares his joy with his friends.

The woman realizes that a coin is missing. The coin had no ability to wander off as did the sheep. It was likely misplaced by the careless action of the woman the last time she handled the coin. She takes responsibility, cleans her house diligently until she finds it, and places it back with the other coins. She shares her joy with her friends.

But the son doesn't wander away aimlessly nor is he misplaced by his father. He chooses to rebel against the father and plot his own course.

The rebellious son's choice to leave was surprisingly honored by the father. He could have forbidden his son to leave or sent others to bring him back, but he didn't. The father bore no responsibility to retrieve the son since leaving was his free choice. The son would have to take the responsibility to return to the father, which he does. After rebellion, remorse, and repentance, joy was found upon the son's return, and it was shared with others.

As the tax collectors and sinners draw to Jesus to hear instruction and truth, the scribes and Pharisees are angry that Jesus would welcome conversations with sinners. They are likely thinking that God takes greater pleasure in punishing the rebellious sinners rather than finding joy in seeing them penitently return. In all three of these parables, we see that the goal is the restoration of the lost.

Going Deeper

Jewish law prescribes that an inheritance be divided with a double portion going to the eldest son (Deut 21:17). In this setting, the younger son would be allotted one-third of the father's goods. It was somewhat common for older fathers to divide their estate while still living, especially if the goal was to provide for the sons to carry on a business while the father retires. However, the way the young son demands the inheritance seems very premature and out of order.

This parable showcases the various stages most people follow when leaving and returning to God: rebellion, remorse, repentance, and restoration.

Rebellion

Rebellion is the initial determination and action to separate from the sovereignty of God and chart a self-serving course. This can be very gradual and subtle or can be immediate and demanding as is the case here.

Not satisfied with the security and abundance the father provides, the young son rebels, with his heart set on finding his own way, following his own rules, and focusing on his own pleasures. His rude demand for his inheritance is granted, and it takes only a few short days before he embarks upon his journey of independence.

He traveled a great distance away from his roots and soon was satisfying his every desire in a very wasteful manner. The objects of his desires were not present in the father's house so he went to where they could be found.

Jesus taught that men loved the cover of darkness because their evil actions would be exposed by the light (John 3:19–21). God, being light, has no darkness in Him (1 John 1:5) so the son's desire to do evil things necessitated that he hide from the light of the father by running to the darkness of a far place.

Remorse

Regret and remorse are very similar in meaning. We can regret a decision, such as eating spicy food too late at night, as we know of the consequences to come. Remorse goes beyond regret and becomes a continuous reminder of the guilt of our wrong choices.

Having satisfied his personal desires, the son discovers that his money has all been spent. His new friends, fond of him when he was paying for the party, have now abandoned him.

Complicating his financial distress, the county entered a severe drought. He found himself desperate to provide for himself and was fortunate to find employment. However, the job he found was to feed swine. A Jewish man was not to have anything to do with unclean animals (Lev 11:7). But this very humiliating and degrading task appears to be his only means to survive if he is to stay on his current route of independence.

Now he finds himself jealous of the food he is feeding to the swine. He regrets his decisions and is remorseful of his dire circumstances.

Repentance

Repentance is when one comprehends mistakes and has a true change of heart toward God. The rebellious young man now clearly sees the mistakes which have led him to his desperate condition. Selfish desires had pulled him away from the father. Pride had kept him away. Now humbled, he embraces the only logical direction to take.

"But when he came to himself" (Luke 15:17a). The Bible teaches us that sin will draw us away from God and entangle us. We become deluded into thinking that life apart from God is just as good if not better than life with God. This verse indicates that the son had a moment of realization where the delusions of sin were diminished, and he could clearly see his path back to the father.

Reminded of the goodness of his father and his ways (Prov 22:6), his genuine grief changed his mind and brought him to action toward his physical salvation (2 Cor 7:10). Knowing he could never make up for the damages he caused, he prepares a humble speech asking the father to take him back as a servant, a day laborer. He knows he is not worthy of any grace or blessing of the father. But he realizes that any position with the father's house is better than any position apart from it. He penitently rises to return to his father.

Restoration

On his journey home the young son probably rehearses his speech for the father, wondering if the father will punish him or accept him as a servant. He has no aspiration of being restored to his former place in the house as a son.

The father has been looking for the son's return and upon seeing him, runs out to greet him. Instead of words of condemnation and punishment, the father covers the son with kisses and immediately sets in order the details for a grand celebration. The penitent speech, humbly rehearsed and refined, is interrupted by the father who gladly welcomes his son home and restores him to his place in the house.

Application

Jesus didn't always refer to sinners as sinners. He often simply referred to them as lost. Had the Pharisees thought more about people as the lost needing to be found instead of sinners needing to be punished, they might have better understood why Jesus spent so much time with people who were accepting of direction, correction, and instruction.

Punishment for wrongdoing and sin is a prescribed fact of the Bible. God does not force us to be obedient or faithful. He warns us of the consequences and leaves the ultimate choice to us.

This parable illustrated that even a rebellious, prideful man can repent and return to God, escaping the punishment and enjoying a restored standing with God. Such is the nature of our loving God who provides mercy, grace, and forgiveness.

People make choices to rebel against God and chart their own course. They will soon find themselves lost in darkness. Pride will blind some and prevent their return to God. Others will welcome direction to find their way back to Him.

Pray that they may all come to their senses, before it is too late, and penitently return to God.

Conclusion

God is more interested in our restoration than our punishment, no matter what we have done and how long we have been away.

> The Lord is not slack concerning His promise, as some count slackness, but is longsuffering toward us, not willing that any should perish but that all should come to repentance (2 Pet 3:9).

Discussion Questions

1. How did selfish desires affect the judgment and desires of the young son? See James 1:13–16.
2. How does pride and stubbornness prevent people from repenting of bad decisions?
3. Why would people fear returning to God and admitting their wrongs?
4. What suggestions would you give in helping others see that God is merciful, and forgiving and really desires for us to return to Him?
5. Have you ever thought that God would enjoy punishing people for sins? How does this parable along with 2 Peter 3:9 change that perception?

Cool Water for a Thirsty Soul
Romans 8:1–31
George Hulett

Focus Passage

ROMANS 8:1–31

One Main Thing

Christians can feel secure in their relationship with the Father.

Introduction

Have you ever watched a toddler begin the process of walking? They pull up on something, then they sway, then they let go, then they fall. Why? Maybe it's because the ground is more than twice as far away as they are used too. Their eyes have gone from a few inches above the floor to two feet above it and the view is very different. They have no problem trying to do this walking thing when mom or dad or big sister is holding their hands. But look at their faces when they realize they are all alone. They are terrified, even while they are excited.

Paul understood that idea when he wrote to the Christians at Rome. This whole Christianity thing was new to them and the idea of failing and falling was just a little scary. So he wrote to encourage them and let them know that they could be secure in the knowledge that God was holding their hands.

Going Deeper

History teaches us that these believers in Rome faced some of the harshest persecution ever recorded. Paul gives several assurances in chapter eight to demonstrate the security of believers and to encourage the Romans in the face of opposition. As we look at a few of these we will notice that the overall premise is to encourage them to continue faithfully in spite of whatever might be going on around them. Let's look at some of these:

No condemnation, none at all, not even a little bit. Paul begins this section of his letter with the bold statement that believers can be secure of their salvation. (Some see this thought as a continuation of the previous chapter and the struggle against sin in our own personal lives. That shouldn't raise any real issues as the entire letter was written to the church and wasn't divided into chapters and verses.) He bases this idea of security upon two premises: if they are "In Christ" and if they "walk by the Spirit." He's already written in chapter six that believers are baptized "into Christ" and that they are no longer slaves to sin but to righteousness — to walk in it.

The Spirit of God dwells in believers. Paul is saying here that God's love for us is so great that He's not satisfied with a long distance relationship. We have been baptized into Christ, and now God, Himself, through His Spirit wishes to walk intimately with us. He wants to share in our thoughts and our lives. That's the great promise Paul is making to the Romans. God is with them — always!

Believers are children of God. Satan is an enemy, and angels are servants, but believers are so much more. Christians are adopted into the family of God. Luke records in Acts 2 that God adds those who are saved to the church. The church is the body, the bride, the kingdom of believers, and the children of God. He goes on to speak of how all of creation has been waiting for this great event.

The Spirit helps with our prayers. How many times have you felt the need to pray, but didn't have the words? "Oh Lord, I don't even know where to begin. Help. Please?" We sometimes find ourselves in situations where we have no idea what to pray for. But the Spirit who dwells in us knows our hearts and takes the desires and hurts and questions to the throne of grace. That's a wonderfully hopeful thing, but it doesn't stop there. The same Spirit returns peace and comfort to us from the throne of grace.

God is on our side. Like David faithfully picking up the stones in the brook, we can face our giants knowing that God will fight our battles for us. When Gideon thinned his army down to 300 men, he trusted that God would be right there with him. Here, Paul reminds us that if God was willing to sacrifice His Son for our sins, He's most assuredly not going to turn His back on us now. When we face our giants and realize that all our strength is not enough, God is on our side. As if God's protection and guidance throughout this life were not enough, Paul even points out that when the time comes for Christians to face judgment, they need not fear because Jesus intercedes for them.

Nothing can separate us from the love of God. Paul ends this section the same way he began it. There's no condemnation. There's nothing that can separate us from God's love. Here are two great truths that Paul understood well: God cannot possibly love you any more than He already does. And God cannot possibly love you any less than He already does. You cannot be so good that God loves you more, and He doesn't love you less when you fail. As a Christian, you are part of God's family and nobody can drag you away against your will. You can choose to deny and give it all up, but even if you build a wall of sin and denial between you, God won't stop loving you. He will let you go, but it breaks His heart to watch you leave.

Application

Christians must continue to live faithfully. In the first chapter of this letter, Paul pointedly reminds the Romans that the Gentiles were guilty of sin. In the next two chapters, he purposely reminds them that Jews were just as guilty of sin as the Gentiles were. Here, he is challenging Christians, those in Christ — whether Jew of Gentile, to continue to live their lives in accordance with God's will. In other words, he wants us to live faithfully. It's not enough to be "In Christ" and not be faithful any more than it was enough to be born a Jew and be unfaithful or be born a Gentile and be a good heathen. We must "walk in the light." That means living in accordance with scripture.

Christ's intercession covers our failures. This is not a license to sin, but a promise of hope.

We, as they, know that we are not without sin. Sometimes the guilt of our past can greatly hamper our relationship with God because we know we are not worthy. Oftentimes ministers counsel with those who say, "You don't understand. I did XYZ, and I just cannot forgive myself."

Number one, you are right — you cannot forgive yourself — you are not God. But, here's the great hope of this entire passage: Christ intercedes for us! We don't deserve it, and we never will. But Jesus chose to intercede on our behalf.

Conclusion

Christians should be able to live calm, confident lives with the assurance that we are in a right relationship with God. This is not some "Once Saved, Always Saved" heresy, but rather an absolute assurance that nothing from outside can interfere with our walk with God. This was especially pertinent to the early church in Rome where much persecution was prevalent. Many of the early readers of this letter would know — or know of — Christians who were abused, abased, and murdered. There was bound to be some fear that their faith might not be strong enough when they personally faced persecution. Paul wanted them to know that God was with them in the face of adversity and that He wasn't going to force them to face these challenges alone. And neither do we face the difficult times in our lives alone.

Paul is saying here that if we are in Christ, nothing can separate us from the love of God. It's not because we don't sin, it's because He never quits loving us. This passage really sheds light on John's words in 1 John 1:7–10 and Jesus's promise that "Lo, I am with you always, even to the end of time." Yes, we can walk away from and deny Him—both Judas and Peter did that. But even if we do, it's still our choice whether to return to Him or to die separated from him. His love for us is constant.

Discussion questions

1. What kinds of challenges to their faith do think the Christians in Rome were facing at this time?
2. How would Paul's assurances give them hope to face their challenges?
3. What challenges do we as Christians face in the world today?
4. How do Paul's words encourage us?

5. What peace or comfort do we derive from God's indwelling Spirit?
6. How does Paul relate the indwelling of the Spirit to our walk with God?
7. What confidences and assurances can we carry forward from these words?

God Shall Wipe Away All Tears
Revelation 21:4
Robert Darby

Focus Passage

And I heard a great voice out of the throne saying, Behold, the tabernacle of God is with men, and he shall dwell with them, and they shall be his peoples, and God himself shall be with them, and be their God: **and He shall wipe away every tear from their eyes;** and death shall be no more; neither shall there be mourning, nor crying, nor pain, any more: the first things are passed away (Rev 21:3–4) ASV.

Introduction

God is a compassionate God. He is concerned with the sadness, suffering, and sins of His people. "But You O Lord, are a God merciful and gracious, slow to anger and abundant in lovingkindness and truth" (Ps 86:15).

Jesus showed His compassionate side while on the earth. Looking upon the city of Jerusalem filled with sin and suffering the scriptures state: "Jesus wept" (Luke 19:41). As His compassion builds near the end of His earthly life He weeps for us as He did for those gathered at the gravesite of Lazarus (John 11:35, Heb 5:7).

God is truly "touched with the feeling of our infirmities" (Heb 4:15).

When we cry, tears fill our eyes. It's an outward sign of our inward suffering. Tears are the result of an emotional pain growing deep within us. When the pain becomes too much to bear, it overflows and comes out the eyes that others will see our pain. God wipes away the tears that reveal the pain within so that we might heal. He touches our hearts to relieve the pain so that we might heal. Why? so there will be no more pain in your world, no more sorrow, only a joyful looking for tomorrow.

When God wipes away the tears, He removes all the pain that has grown through the years. He removes all the heartaches that hinder us from drawing close to Him. It humbles our minds that a God so powerful could be so compassionate.

God in His compassion sought to inform us that it will be alright. So, He commissioned the apostle John to send us the word that Jesus knows and that Jesus cares.

John, the disciple whom Jesus loved, was exiled on Patmos's isle and told to write the things he saw in a book. For twenty chapters he wrote to encourage the church by enlightening them of the things that shortly must come to pass (Rev 1).

In chapter twenty one he begins to conclude this

great book. He takes us to one final scene; he takes us home. To the shores of Heaven and the comforting hands of God as He promises to make all things right. The end of our earthly sojourn is described in 1 Thessalonians 4: 13–18 and 2 Thessalonians 1:7–10, and the redeemed enter the Heavenly realm (Rev 20:11–15).

When chapter 21 begins we find these words, "And I saw a new heaven and a new earth: for the first heaven and the first earth were passed away; and there was no more sea." On the third day of Creation God created the first heaven(s) and the earth. The heaven and the earth, were filled with living creatures, and the sea were populated with all manner of fish (Gen 1: 9–13). In the day of judgment, heaven and earth, called the first, shall be destroyed, and as an added note he writes, and there were no more sea (Rev 21:1).

There will be no so-called rapture. God's plan is one day of judgment for all, for all time. The earth will be destroyed. Jesus said: "Heaven and earth shall pass away, but my word will never pass away" (Matt 24:35). Jesus encourages His disciples by saying:

> Let not your heart be troubled, believe in God, believe also in Me. For in my Father's house are many mansions. If it were not so, I would have told you. I go and prepare a place for you, and if I go I will come again and receive you unto myself, that where I am, there you may be also (John 14:1–3).

Be not troubled in your heart, there is room for you,

for all who trust in God through His Son. For heaven is a prepared place, for those prepared to go.

Now John enters the pearly portals and stands near the throne. The great throne room of heaven. The place where God is manifest before the presence of the church, the called-out assembly. It is a scene of grandeur, greatness, and glory.

The dwelling place of God has always been with man and for man. For God chose a people to be His, and He chose to be with them. For our Father God is concerned with our welfare, our physical, mental, and spiritual being. And, if it is just a tear, God will wipe it from our eyes.

We shall know death no more, nor the things associated with death. No more mourning, no more crying. No more pain. For the former things are passed away.

Going Deeper

Man is a threefold creature. He is body, mind, and soul. When we speak of the weakness of man, we must address his true nature. The body, the mind, and then the soul (the physical, mental, and spiritual being).

Our eyes shed a tear when the heart feels pain. In an attempt to counsel the weary hearts of a once wicked man, God talks about another place that gives us a second chance for a beneficial life. John writes: There shall be a new heaven and a new earth. The old one is to pass away. The new one is here to stay. The new city is called Jerusalem [the name consists of two elements, "yrw" pronounced, "Jeru" (foundations or city) and "Salem" which is the name of deity (thus the City of God)]. While speaking of Abraham and his faith, Hebrews says: "For he looked for the city which hath foundations, whose builder and maker is God" (Heb 11:10).

The new heaven is to come down from God and be the dwelling place of God among men. It's not to literally come down to the old earth's location, but it is to be revealed to man on his level.

God will dwell with man, and man shall dwell with God. He will be our God, and we shall be the people of His heart.

God Himself shall heal His people. No more pain, no more suffering. The things that we knew made us blue and caused our hearts to cry out to God who heals.

God uses the word "all" which means a complete wiping of the tears through the years, and past all the fears. God, Himself, shall personally wipe away all of our tears. All things are passed away. The things that bound us and kept us from knowing the joy of living for God. We shall dwell in the land of "No More." No more trials or tribulations. No more punishment, no more pain. No more tears.

Application

God will not have us to be ignorant. He shares with those for whom He cares. An enlightened heart is a living heart. David wrote: "Consider and hear me, O Lord my God: Lighten mine eyes, lest I sleep of death" (Ps 13:3). To enlighten is to deliver us from the gloom of doom to the joy of the knowledge of God. For in sickness and grief, the eyes are dull and heavy, but health and joy will bring back the brightness and sparkle in our eyes. Spiritual light enlightens the soul. "For Thou will light my candle: the Lord my God will enlighten my darkness" (Ps 18:28). To know is to grow. God desires that we know, so as His people, we can grow. "Grow in the grace and knowledge of our Lord and Savior Jesus Christ. To Him be the glory both now and forever" (2 Pet 3:18).

Conclusion

One verse of scripture that while taken in context can be so meaningful to so many people. It speaks of the *Power of God*. Man has used many things of this world to comfort and console himself. Some men drink to forget their problems. Some smoke to allow their thoughts to be carried away. Others use drugs to help them forget the feelings and the foes that haunt their thoughts each day.

This verse also speaks of the *Presence of God*. God draws near the troubled in heart. He touches our lives through His word. He eases our pains through His eternal touch.

Finally, this verse speaks of the *Provisions of God*. God cares. "He is not willing that any should perish, but that all should come to repentance" (2 Pet 3:9). God our Creator, is our Redeemer, and Sustainer of life (Acts 17:24).

Discussion Questions

1. Why are the tears of mankind important to God?
2. How will God remove or wipe away our tears?
3. Does this apply to past as well as present tears.?
4. Is this promise to all the children of God?

Sharing our Blessings
John 13:34–35
Jerry R. Self

DID YOU EVER HEAR SOMEONE SAY, "I DIDN'T GET much out of church today?" Perhaps some of us have even been heard to make such a statement. Are we truly aware how sad this reflects on our relationship with God and others? Reflect on our eagerness to show photos of our kids and grandkids. Love to talk about them. Do we love the Lord enough to talk about Him with others?

In our text Jesus said His people should be identifiable by their hearts filled with love. He said, "love one another; as I have loved you, that ye also love one another. By this shall all *men* know that ye are my disciples, if ye have love one to another" (John 13:34–35).

After Jesus had silenced the Sadducees on one occasion, a Pharisee who was a lawyer came to Him and asked,

> Master, which *is* the great commandment in the law?
> Jesus said unto him, Thou shalt love the Lord thy God

with all thy heart, and with all thy soul, and with all thy mind. This is the first and great commandment. And the second *is* like unto it, Thou shalt love thy neighbour as thyself (Matt 22:36–39).

The lawyer here is an expert in the law of Moses, not the law of Rome.

The Bible says,

For God so loved the world, that he gave his only begotten Son, that whosoever believeth in him should not perish, but have everlasting life (John 3:16).

John declares,

We love him, because he first loved us. If a man say, I love God, and hateth his brother, he is a liar: for he that loveth not his brother whom he hath seen, how can he love God whom he hath not seen? (1 John 4:19–20).

Writing to the Corinthian Christians, Paul speaks of one household who has addicted themselves to the gospel (1 Cor 16:15). *Addicted is defined as*, "physically and mentally dependent on a particular substance, and unable to stop taking it without incurring adverse effects." In this case, that to which they were addicted was the gospel. They were addicted to God's word and to sharing it with others.

Therefore, it is abundantly clear from these verses

that to be a disciple of Christ, and to go to heaven, a Christian must have two passions—one for Christ and one for his fellow man. These two passions are what Christianity is about.

God First

Jesus commanded, "But seek ye first the kingdom of God, and his righteousness; and all these things shall be added unto you" (Matt 6:33).

Jesus made it abundantly clear that God must come first in the life of the Christian. This was quite clear in His response to the question He was asked regarding the greatest commandment.

> Jesus said unto him, Thou shalt love the Lord thy God with all thy heart, and with all thy soul, and with all thy mind. This is the first and great commandment. And the second *is* like unto it, Thou shalt love thy neighbour as thyself (Matt 22:37–39).

Notice that He gave not only the first commandment but also the second. Jesus insisted that those who would be His disciples must not only place God first in their lives, but they also had a great responsibility toward others. There is no place for selfishness in our lives if we are to be Christians.

> A new commandment I give unto you, That ye love one another; as I have loved you, that ye also love one

another. By this shall all *men* know that ye are my disciples, if ye have love one to another (John 13:34–35).

In Jesus's prayer to the Father, He prayed for His disciples.

Sanctify them through thy truth: thy word is truth. As thou hast sent me into the world, even so have I also sent them into the world. And for their sakes I sanctify myself, that they also might be sanctified through the truth. Neither pray I for these alone, but for them also which shall believe on me through their word; That they all may be one; as thou, Father, *art* in me, and I in thee, that they also may be one in us: that the world may believe that thou hast sent me (John 17:17–21).

Paul explained to the Colossians that if we are Christians, Christ must be our life.

If ye then be risen with Christ, seek those things which are above, where Christ sitteth on the right hand of God. Set your affection on things above, not on things on the earth. For ye are dead, and your life is hid with Christ in God. When Christ, *who is* our life, shall appear, then shall ye also appear with him in glory (Col 3:1–4).

That is exactly what Paul practiced. To the Galatians, he said,

I am crucified with Christ: nevertheless I live; yet not I, but Christ liveth in me: and the life which I now live in the flesh I live by the faith of the Son of God, who loved me, and gave himself for me (Gal 2:20).

People-Centered

Not only is Christianity to be totally "God first" focused, but it is also to be people focused as well.

Notice that when asked about the first commandment, Jesus gave the second commandment with it. He said to love God and love thy neighbor. He emphasized the part of love and unity among His disciples as an identifying characteristic of those who followed Him. The great work He gave His apostles of getting God's saving gospel to the world also identified the place of others in the lives of Christians.

Of One Heart and One Soul

When benevolence was needed,

And the multitude of them that believed were of one heart and of one soul: neither said any *of them* that ought of the things which he possessed was his own; but they had all things common. And with great power gave the apostles witness of the resurrection of the Lord Jesus: and great grace was upon them all. Neither was there any among them that lacked: for as many as were possessors of lands or houses sold them, and brought the prices of the things that were sold,

And laid *them* down at the apostles' feet: and distribution was made unto every man according as he had need. And Joses, who by the apostles was surnamed Barnabas, (which is, being interpreted, The son of consolation,) a Levite, *and* of the country of Cyprus, Having land, sold *it,* and brought the money, and laid *it* at the apostles' feet (Acts 4:32–37).

Back in Acts chapter 4 we saw their zeal, commitment to Christ, and to each other. Many were selling possessions and distributing to all who had need. Immediately following the days of public and private teaching in the Temple and in every house, the Bible declares the rapid growth of the church as Christianity spread rapidly. People were hearing the gospel of Jesus's death, burial, and resurrection, and were responding to it.

And in those days, when the number of the disciples was multiplied, there arose a murmuring of the Grecians against the Hebrews, because their widows were neglected in the daily ministration. Then the twelve called the multitude of the disciples *unto them,* and said, It is not reason that we should leave the word of God, and serve tables. Wherefore, brethren, look ye out among you seven men of honest report, full of the Holy Ghost and wisdom, whom we may appoint over this business. But we will give ourselves continually to prayer, and to the ministry of the word (Acts 6:1–4).

Nothing was going to prevent or slow their missionary zeal in sharing the saving gospel of Christ with others. However, they understood also that their passion for saving the souls of men could not cause them to neglect the physical needs of others. They truly did love their neighbors as themselves (Matt 22:39).

So enraged by Stephen's preaching Jesus, a mob stoned him. The Bible says,

> But he, being full of the Holy Ghost, looked up stedfastly into heaven, and saw the glory of God, and Jesus standing on the right hand of God, And said, Behold, I see the heavens opened, and the Son of man standing on the right hand of God. Then they cried out with a loud voice, and stopped their ears, and ran upon him with one accord, And cast *him* out of the city, and stoned *him:* and the witnesses laid down their clothes at a young man's feet, whose name was Saul. And they stoned Stephen, calling upon *God,* and saying, Lord Jesus, receive my spirit. And he kneeled down, and cried with a loud voice, Lord, lay not this sin to their charge. And when he had said this, he fell asleep (Acts 7:55–60).

His passion for Christ, and for their lost souls, was so great that he died rather than fail to share the saving gospel with them. Even in death, he expressed forgiveness to God for what they were doing to him. This is first-century New Testament Christianity in its purity!

Did their being persecuted as a result of their sharing

the gospel of Jesus discourage the disciples from their mission? No. They continued to preach Christ. Did the stoning to death of Stephen slow down the disciples' zeal in telling of the death, burial, and resurrection of Jesus? No!

Enthusiasm

Paul affirmed that in his life, "For to me to live *is* Christ, and to die *is* gain" (Phil 1:21).

> I am crucified with Christ: nevertheless I live; yet not I, but Christ liveth in me: and the life which I now live in the flesh I live by the faith of the Son of God, who loved me, and gave himself for me (Gal 2:20).

The Psalmist said, "I was glad when they said unto me, Let us go into the house of the LORD" (Ps 122:1).

Discussion Questions

1. How do we react to each other when we assemble for worship? When we are away from our assemblies?
2. Compare our group loyalties in time spent with Christians? With others? Support of each other in time of need?
3. Do we attend worship only for the sake of our own spiritual life and personal salvation, or for the sharing of our faith with others?

4. Discuss Jesus's statement about loving our enemies. Compare and contrast how hard to control feelings versus controlling actions. Include the idea of "love" as an action/feeling.

New Exodus Led by Christ
Matthew 2–4
Jordan Gray

Jesus said to him, "I am the way, and the truth, and the life. No one comes to the Father except through me.
John 14:6

The Way Out

BACK BEFORE COMMON CORE AND GOOGLE, I WAS taught to keep the personal pronoun out of writings such as this one, but seeing as this is a chapter about my favorite text, I'll relent for a moment. I've always had a fascination for literary architecture. That is, I am endlessly fascinated by the masterful techniques of the biblical Storyteller, as He fits each passage and pericope just so, weaving a grand, unified epic out of thousands of individual strands. I worship His genius as He draws the story of sacrificial son forward from Moriah to Calvary; as He tells the story of circumcision from Abraham to Colossians; as He carries the Tree of Life from Eden to

Ezekiel, and on into John's Celestial City. In short, the Bible moves me most profoundly when through it I see how *all things* are written by Him, to Him, and for Him. You and I, reader, are but single poems — all at once new and ancient — singing a song in harmony with Abraham, Isaac, and Jacob.

It is in this light that I turn to the new and ancient story of Exodus, viewed from three vantage points: (1) the story of ancient Israel, (2) the life of Christ as recorded in Matthew 2–4, and (3) our own, unique life experiences. In it, we will experience the powerful continuity of the Bible, as we are personally drawn into one of the most foundational narratives in Scripture through the model of our Lord Jesus Himself – He who said, "I AM the Way" (John 14:6). Interestingly, the Greek word "exodus" literally means "way" (or, more specifically, "way out"). As was foretold, Jesus is the prophet like Moses (Deut 18:15), leading a New Exodus out of slavery and into the Promised Land, as He is Himself "the Way."

As we examine this way, asking what it means for our own journeys of faith, let's start at the beginning with a quick summary of the first Exodus in four basic movements.

The Exodus of Ancient Israel

It's easy to forget that "Israel," for the most part, was just a personal name before Egypt. Aside from an editorial note (Gen 32:32), the term "people of Israel" doesn't pick up until Exodus 1:7, where we see that Jacob's family has become a distinct people group. It is here in Egypt that a nation is born, and it is here that God begins to shape the identity of His chosen people, speaking forth (as it were) an immortal story of bondage, deliverance, becoming, and priesthood.

BONDAGE

Israel's journey begins in the most likely and unlikely of places. Considering the Creator of Heaven and Earth had promised Abram, "I will make of you a great nation, and I will bless you and make your name great" (Gen 12:2), who would have thought that this great and blessed nation would be formed under oppression? Just imagine the surprise Abram must have felt as God expounded upon the promise, revealing that His people would first experience slavery 400 years (Gen 15:13)!

On the other hand, it makes perfect sense that our story would begin in slavery. The default state of being in our fallen world — the status quo — is bondage. We live in a world in which sin has obscured the Tree of Life, while man's choice to define right and wrong for himself has ushered in the promised death (Gen 2:17). In this world, men use and abuse one another, and all are oppressed by the deceitful powers of darkness. It only makes sense that God's people would find bondage in a world such as this, as bondage finds us all eventually.

It's worth noting that Israel merely does that which makes sense when he makes an alliance with the powerful Egyptian nation (Gen 47). By the hand of God, the favor of worldly power and success is showered upon the young man Joseph and his family, and a mutually beneficial partnership is forged. However, the powers of this world do what they will always do, and Israel is ultimately betrayed into bondage.

DELIVERANCE

It must be remembered that Israel was powerless to escape bondage. In the face of suffocating oppression, Israel had no answer, no might, no cunning, no strategy. The one and only response they could muster was a *groan*: "And the people of Israel groaned because of their slavery and cried out for help" (Exod 2:23). Israel had no recourse for bondage; Israel had to be saved. And, in due time, God "saved them for his name's sake, that he might make known his mighty power" (Ps 106:8).

And, what a salvation it was! The most powerful nation in the world reeled as God sent judgment after judgment. Decades later, the neighboring nations still confessed, "The fear of you has fallen upon us ... for we have heard how the LORD dried up the water of the Red Sea before you" (Josh 2:9–10). God saved His people, drawing them from oppression into freedom, and doing so with such unquestionable power that the world indeed knew His name.

BECOMING

Of course, God was not concerned merely with relocating His people; God desired to build His people. And so, God took Israel into the wilderness, where He led them through a season of becoming. They camped at Sinai, where He taught them His ways. He taught them to worship. He taught them how to channel their gifts and energies into a relationship with Himself, knowing that therein lay the source of life.

Not only did God build Israel up in the wilderness, He also stripped them down, working out their fears and idolatries. Israel earns its name in the wilderness, "striving with God" (Gen 32:28), and navigating the hard questions, "Can this God be trusted? Will we devote our whole selves to this God? Will we still follow this God in seasons of hardship? Even when His commands seemingly make no sense?"

If God freed Israel externally at the Red Sea, He freed them internally in the wilderness. At the Red Sea, God brought Israel out of Egypt; in the wilderness, He brought Egypt out of Israel. He led them to *become* that which He saved them to be.

PRIESTHOOD

And, what did God save Israel to be? "You shall be my treasured possession among all the peoples... a kingdom of priests and a holy nation" (Ex 19:5–6). From the very start, God had a purpose in mind for Israel. To Abram, He'd promised, "In you all the families of the earth shall be blessed" (Gen 12:3). God was leading

Israel in an exodus from Egypt to Canaan, not just for Israel's sake, but for the world's sake. And, even years later, through apostasy and exile, God's vision for Israel remained the same, "and nations shall come to your light, and kings to the brightness of your rising" (Isa 60:3).

Israel was saved from bondage through the gracious deliverance of a powerful God, formed by a challenging journey of faith, that they might serve as priests — a light to the world, blessing all families of the earth.

Jesus: An Israelite Indeed

Tragically, we come now to our text in Matthew 2–4 with the understanding that Israel failed to be that kingdom of priests God envisioned. There were, of course, some bright moments along the way, but by and large, Israel actually regressed into bondage once more. God's people were again groaning, waiting upon the consolation of Israel (Luke 2:25) — the restoration of the kingdom (Acts 1:6).

Enter Jesus of Nazareth

The fascinating thing about Israel's Messiah, however, is that He doesn't descend out of the clouds with chariots of fire and peals of thunder. He doesn't subdue the Roman Empire with plagues of judgment and sea-splitting ferocity. His power is unquestionable and His short campaign fundamentally shifts the entire universe, but consider the approach of Christ as He enters into the very story Israel had been called to demonstrate — how He takes up the calling of an Israelite Himself and perfectly embodies everything that Israel had failed to be.

BONDAGE

> *[Joseph] rose and took the child and his mother by night and departed to Egypt and remained there until the death of Herod. This was to fulfill what the Lord had spoken by the prophet, "Out of Egypt I called my son"* (Matt 2:14–15).

From the flight to and from Egypt to the murder of the innocents, Matthew 2 is a tragic reminder that the world hadn't changed a bit since Pharoah. Death's curse had not lifted, and earth's status quo remained the same — bondage.

Remarkably, however, a conquering Light shines in the darkness (John 1:5). A Child is born, and a Son is given (Isa 9:6). God Himself takes on flesh and visits His people, not by stepping over the darkness, but by *entering into the bondage Himself.* The cold realities of oppression and poverty and violence strike at Him just as they've struck at every other Israelite. He feels the strictures in His own body of the broken flesh. In every respect, Jesus enters into the weaknesses of a people under bondage (Heb 4:15).

DELIVERANCE

When Jesus was baptized, immediately he went up from the water, and behold, the heavens were opened to him, and he saw the Spirit of God descending like a dove and coming to rest on him; and behold, a voice from heaven said, "This is my beloved Son, with whom I am well pleased" (Matt 3:16–17).

Whatever might be said of the nuances involved in Christ's baptism, Paul made a point to cast the Red Sea deliverance as a baptism event, in which, Christ was present (1 Cor 10:1–4). Matthew (who very likely has read the Corinthian letters before writing his Gospel account) highlights Jesus's own Red Sea moment, positioned here between the bondage of Chapter 2 and the becoming of Chapter 4.

No, Jesus did not experience a baptism deliverance in the same way we might think of it today, but notice the four pivotal changes Jesus did experience in baptism. It was a moment of *transition,* as Jesus goes from one phase of His life to the next. It was a *commencement,* marking the beginning of Jesus's ministry. It was a moment of *empowerment,* as the Holy Spirit came to rest on Him. It was marked with an *identification,* as the Father said, "This is My Son."

BECOMING

Then Jesus was led up by the Spirit into the wilderness to be tempted by the devil. And after fasting forty days and forty nights, he was hungry (Matt 4:1–2).

Just as God proved Israel for forty years in the wilderness, Jesus is tried and tested for forty days in His own season of becoming. Moses spoke to Israel, "God has led you these forty years in the wilderness, that he might humble you, testing you to know what was in your heart, whether you would keep his commandments or not" (Deut 8:2). In the wilderness, we see precisely what is in Jesus's heart as He clings to God in humility.

As the tempter presses upon Him with visions of miracle bread, Jesus doesn't simply quote Deuteronomy 8; everything about Him is living Deuteronomy 8, as He "lives by every word that comes from the mouth of God" (Deut 8:3). If the Israelites were humbled by eating manna, Jesus epitomizes humility by forgoing it, relying solely on the essence of heavenly bread — God Himself.

PRIESTHOOD

> *From that time Jesus began to preach, saying, "Repent,*
> *for the kingdom of heaven is at hand"* (Matt 4:17).

From the wilderness of becoming, Jesus emerges into His ministry. Day in and day out, without fail, He led a life of God-given purpose. He called, He taught, He healed, He confronted, He worshipped, He loved, He reconciled, He died, He rose. Jesus sought not His own pleasure and well-being, but emptied Himself in obedience (Phil 2:5–11). He came into the world, saying, "I have come to do your will, O God" (Heb 10:5–7). Everything about Him was brought into the service of God,

which is why all nations will be blessed through Him
(Gen 12:3) and all nations will come to His light (Isa
60:3). He is our great High Priest (Heb 4:14).

A New Exodus in Christ

To bring it all home, we now must recognize that the
triumphant path of Christ, which was the reluctant path
of Israel, is now the path of our calling. We too have been
called out of bondage, through deliverance, into seasons
of becoming, to emerge as a royal priesthood.

My story begins in bondage. *My* story. Say it right
now and own it, because it is critically important that we
receive the Gospel! Terrible things happen to those who
cannot (or will not) claim their bondage. When Jesus
spoke of freedom, the response came back rather
obtusely, "We are offspring of Abraham and have never
been enslaved to anyone. How is it that you say, 'You will
become free'?" (John 8:33). The Pharisees took issue with
Jesus's charge of blindness, to which He gave a chilling
assessment, "If you were blind, you would have no guilt;
but now that you say, 'We see,' your guilt remains" (John
9:41). To disclaim our bondage is to blind ourselves to the
power of the Gospel as we remain in the guilt of our sins.
Let us cry out instead — let us *groan* — "God, be merciful
to me, a sinner" (Luke 18:13)!

Praise God, my story is a story of deliverance. When
I had nothing but a groan, He heard me. When I had no
remedy, He saved me. Crushing the powers of sin and
death, Jesus made the world know His name as He

judged Death itself and brought me safely through the waters. And now, in my baptism, I've experienced a great *transition*. A new life has *commenced*. The Holy Spirit *empowers* me from within, and I have been *identified* — beloved son of God.

Of course, God does not merely desire to relocate His children. Not only has He "transferred us to the kingdom of his beloved Son" (Col 1:13), He is transforming us into the image of the Son by the power of the Spirit (2 Cor 3:18). Before you get too excited, however, understand that the wilderness is essential to the Christian's becoming. It is not in human nature to simply let go of Egypt; our hearts must be stripped down and rebuilt in seasons of testing. The Hebrew writer counts it "fitting" that even Jesus would be made "perfect through suffering," noting that "he who sanctifies and those who are sanctified all have one source" (Heb 2:10–11). Even in the most difficult trials, Christians are called to embrace the wilderness where our hearts are revealed and refined by fire (1 Pet 1:6–7).

And, please don't miss this, every good exodus has a destination. God does not simply lead us out, He leads us *to*. We have not been delivered and sanctified for our own pleasure and well-being. We have been bought at great cost to glorify God (1 Cor 6:20)! We are His "holy priesthood... "offer[ing] spiritual sacrifices acceptable to God through Jesus Christ" (1 Pet 2:5). To us, He has given the ministry of reconciliation (2 Cor 5:18), such that all nations might be blessed through the Body of Christ — His Church (Gen 12:3; Acts 13:47). As Christians, we have not been saved to wait on Heaven; we've been saved to lead lives that declare the good news of the Kingdom of Heaven (Matt 4:17).

The Way Forward

Bondage. Deliverance. Becoming. Priesthood.

It's the whole story of the Bible in four words. The reluctant path of Israel has been redeemed as the triumphant path of Christ, and it is the path of the Christian's calling — the New Exodus. As disciples who have pledged to follow the Master in all things, let us dedicate our whole lives to His example, as "He is the head of the body, the church. He is the beginning, the firstborn from the dead, that in everything he might be preeminent" (Col 1:18).

Discussion Questions

1. In what ways am I tempted to deny my bondage today? Instead of denying the "Egypt" God is still working out of me, how I can receive and glorify the Gospel in my life?

2. If our deliverance is God's gift of transition, commencement, Holy Spirit empowerment, and identification, which one of those words means the most to me? Which do I struggle most to receive?

3. How has God led (or how is He presently leading) me to "become" through seasons of

wilderness? How might we guard against these becoming seasons of despair instead of seasons of growth?

4. How is Jesus blessing me to reign and mediate in His Kingdom today?

Access
Luke 11:9–10
Bryan Collins

You may remember way back in the late 1970's or early 1980's when they were planning a royal wedding in England. There have been two more that made national headlines since then. There have been numerous tragedies and embarrassments for the crown since then as well, which have not escaped the international media. The question need not be asked, who among us received an invitation or waited anxiously for such an invitation to any of these events be they weddings or funerals. The truth of this is not because you are not worthy but simply because you lack such access.

Although, many may have watched these spectacles as they were widely televised here in the United States. All the major networks suspended reporting national events to cover the wedding of Charles and Diana, William and Kate, and Harry and Megan. The same is true of the Queen's funeral procession. Some of you reading this may have been on a vacation or booked flights to be one in the crowd to witness one or more of these processions because of an interest you had in these affairs. However, it is unlikely that any of you attended as an invited guests because you do not have the necessary access. Forgive me, I do not intend to offend you. I do not know what has to take place; what are the protocols for an audience with a Queen, a King, or any other royal. I doubt that I ever will know that process because I do not have access. A monarchy is beyond my comprehension to a degree and it does not fit my life context.

I have never had an audience with a president, and I do not know how to go about that because I do not have access. I have no access to United States Representatives. When I write a letter to my congressman, I get a response in the form of a form letter with a printed signature. If I call a congressional office I am sure I will be reassured that my message will be "relayed" to the congressperson. Yet, I know that this is not likely to happen because I do not have the required access. When fighting my own immigration battle many people around me wanted to be helpful and tried to touch their contact points or their access points with senators and congressmen all of whom were impotent seemingly because their access was an illusion or worse, my case was unremarkable, I was not worthy of the favor because I am not wealthy, influential, or powerful.

Before I digress into a political tirade I only mention these points for purposes of illustration; to illustrate a spiritual point. While you may lack access to so-called powerful people on this earth, have you ever considered the access you have to the most powerful individual in existence? Have you ever considered the fact that you can, at your will and convenience, speak to the most high God?

Open your Bible to Luke 11:9–10 and notice what these verses convey to you:

> So I say to you, seek, and you will find; knock, and it
> will be opened to you. For everyone who seeks, finds
> and to him who knocks it will be opened.

If you believe the Bible is true, God has revealed a powerful secret to you. You have open access, through prayer, to God. This is no small thing. Let's take a few minutes and consider the implications this has for our lives.

First of all, through prayer, you have open access, anytime day or night to the creator of the world. Genesis 1 tells how God spoke everything into existence by the power of His voice and that all of it was good. Then John wrote of the Word that became flesh who was in the beginning with God and says of Him that not one thing came into being that has come into being apart from Him (John 1:2). Going back to Genesis 2:7, which says that the Almighty breathed into the nostrils of the man He made and He came to life. Who cares about access to royals or politicians when you've got that kind of access? What could we accomplish if we organized ourselves around that idea?

Through prayer, you have access to the King of Kings and the Lord of Lords. As stated above, I personally, have no understanding of the protocol for appearing before a royal or a nationally known politician here in the U.S.

When it comes to monarchy and royalty it is not exactly an open door. Consider the biblical examples we have of such things. Esther was reluctant to use her limited access to her own husband (Esth 4:11), she was not allowed to go to him to chat unless she had been called, and anyone who made it into the king's throne room was likely to be killed on the spot unless the king held out his scepter. Nehemiah, the king's cupbearer was anxious and afraid about his physical and facial appearance in front of the king because if he appeared sad the king might dismiss him or worse, Nehemiah chapter 2. Nathan took his life into his own hands when he confronted King David over his sins with Bathsheba. David was once afraid when running from King Saul of what would happen if he was not seated in his regular spot at the king's table. The conclusion has to be that there is no such thing as a casual relationship with a monarch. This is also true of prominent and influential people. You must take care in such relations. Yet, because of our lack of experience and knowledge, we do not understand the access that we have been granted by God to speak to Him.

Matthew 7:7 likewise reads, "Ask, and it will be given to you; seek, and you will find; knock, and it will be opened to you." Going on a few verses, Matthew 7:11 states, "If you then, being evil, know how to give good gifts to your children, how much more will your Father who is in heaven give good things to those who ask Him!" In the same vein, Mark 11:24 states, "Therefore I say to you, whatever things you ask when you pray, believe that you receive them, and you will have them." This same idea is repeated throughout the Scriptures more times than I can outline in one lesson. Your King has not only welcomed you with open arms into His throne room He has commanded you to open your heart and pour your every concern out to Him to have Him take care of it for you. An interesting passage from the Hebrew writer speaks to this idea. Hebrews 4:14–16 reveals to us,

> Seeing then that we have a great High Priest who has passed through the heavens, Jesus the Son of God, let us hold fast our confession. For we do not have a High Priest who cannot sympathize with our weaknesses, but was in all points tempted as we are, yet without sin. Let us therefore come boldly to the throne of grace, that we may obtain mercy and find grace to help in time of need.

A word of caution is deserved here, there is a protocol. When you consider the fact that when we pray we are before the King of Kings and the Lord of Lords; the almighty God you cannot but bow your head and fall on your knees. Remember Isaiah's reaction to his vision of the Lord in Isaiah 6:5, "Woe is me, I am undone!" Isaiah realized his place before the sovereign God of the universe. When we consider what it is we have in the "avenue" of prayer, it should fill us with gratitude: we suddenly realize the blessings of the things we take for granted. What do the five senses mean to you, and how valuable are they? What is it worth in terms of wealth to be able to walk? What does it mean to have food, clothes, shelter, climate control, ability to pay the bills? This understanding fills me with new hope and vigor that I have access to the One who saves, the One who has been involved in world affairs. That is why we call it "history" because it is all "His Story." The protocol is to bow, thank, and plead. This gives grace and mercy new meaning does it not?

Through prayer, you have access to and involvement in the one kingdom that will surely endure. God's kingdom has an open border! You have been invited regardless of background, past, race, or gender. You have been invited to become part of a kingdom that embraces all nations and tongues. He understands all the languages of man and accepts all colors and cultures as long as one obeys. You are judged on the basis of your heart. There is no paperwork, no hassle, and no exorbitant fees to pay. More importantly, God's kingdom will never fail or be overthrown. In 2 Peter 1:10–11, the apostle stated by inspiration,

> Therefore, brethren, be even more diligent to make your call and election sure, for if you do these things you will never stumble; for so an entrance will be supplied to you abundantly into the everlasting kingdom of our Lord and Savior Jesus Christ.

Unlike the kingdoms of the world, the kingdom of God will never go broke. It will not rob your pension plan, it will not run a deficit or create unfunded mandates, and there will be no recession or depression. What's more, there will be no shortage of places to live; there are many dwelling places with no threat of a "bubble market." Jesus said so in John 14:2–3. There is a place there for you that He has prepared for you. God's kingdom cannot be overthrown from within or without, Hebrews 12:25–29 reassures us,

> See that you do not refuse Him who speaks. For if they did not escape who refused Him who spoke on earth, much more shall we not escape if we turn away from Him who speaks from heaven, whose voice shook the earth; but now He has promised, saying, "Yet once more I shake not only the earth, but also heaven." Now this, "Yet once more," indicates the removal of those things that are being shaken, as of things that are made, tha the things which cannot be shaken may remain. Therefore, since we are receiving a kingdom which cannot be shaken, let us have grace, by which we may serve God acceptably with reverence and godly fear. For our God is a consuming fire.

My hope is that these thoughts will help you renew your appreciation and dependence upon prayer and that you will devote yourself to prayer. Paul told the Thessalonians (1 Thess 5:17), "pray without ceasing." He told Timothy (1 Tim 2:8), "I desire therefore that the men pray everywhere, lifting up holy hands, without wrath and doubting." James wrote that we ought to pray in times of suffering, James 5:13, and that the prayers of a righteous man are powerful, James 5:18. Peter wrote, 1 Peter 4:7, "But the end of all things is at hand; therefore be serious and watchful in your prayers."

*All Scriptures that appear in this lesson are from the NKJV.

Discussion Questions

1. Why does the Almighty grant us access to His heart and will?
2. Are there any potential dangers in speaking of prayer as access to God?
3. Why would the devil want us to doubt our access to God?
4. How might the devil tempt us to misuse our wondrous access to our Father?
5. How can we best imitate God's example of offering access to weak and flawed creatures?
6. How can we best show our appreciation to God for granting us access to His throne?

No Condemnation!
Romans 8:1–11
Chris Carrillo

Introduction

ROMANS 8 IS A SUBSECTION OF PAUL'S ARGUMENT and a partial explanation of what it means to be found in Christ. To fully appreciate this argument, one must read the preceding chapters in their entirety. Paul is writing to the brethren in Rome to teach them about the grace of God. More than just the idea of the grace of God, Paul is explaining how to access this grace. Romans 8:1–11 discusses the necessity of having the Spirit of God within the Christian.

As Paul explains the necessity of the Spirit of God in the life of a Christian, he frames the argument by comparing the flesh and the Spirit. The verbiage for flesh and Spirit changes throughout the text, yet the argument remains the same. He opens the 8th chapter with the following two verses:

There is therefore now no condemnation for those who are in Christ Jesus. For the law of the Spirit of life has set you free in Christ Jesus from the law of sin and death.

Paul opens this section of the argument by discussing the law of the Spirit of life and the law of sin and death. This law of sin and death is not the Mosaic law, but rather it is the moral compass of those who do not rely upon God for their salvation. It is the choices people make and the actions they take that are sinful. Thus, their actions become a law unto them. The end of chapter seven attests to the goodness of the Mosaic law and to the sinfulness of man. How are we to be free of this sinful reality? The answer lies in, and only in, Jesus Christ.

Going Deeper

Why does Paul deem it necessary to mention that there is no condemnation in Christ Jesus? It must be because outside of Christ there is condemnation. If this is the case, then there must be a way to be found in Christ. If there's a way to be found in Christ, then there must also be a way to verify this. Based on Paul's comparison of the two different laws, that of the Spirit of life and that of sin and death, it seems obvious that the Spirit leads to life and sin leads to death. This is a part of Paul's complete argument as we can read from Romans 3:23 and 6:23. These two verses are part of the supporting argument leading up to verse 8:1.

This gift that comes from being in Christ, what

exactly does it do? Paul mentions that there is no condemnation for those who are "in Christ," yet, what does that mean? In looking at the 3rd verse of chapter 8, we can begin to understand how this gift applies to us. As people, we have all committed sin. To be found righteous in God's eyes, there can be no sin within us. What exactly did Jesus's death on the cross accomplish? Certainly, it was the forgiveness of sins (Acts 2:38), but how were the sins forgiven? Well, Paul explains that Jesus condemned sin!

By condemning sin, Jesus found sin to be unworthy of our lives. Jesus found sin to be unworthy of humans! So, when we are found in Christ, our sin which leads to death has been condemned and expelled from us. This is how we can fulfill the righteous requirement of the law because it is not us who is fulfilling it, but rather Jesus who has already fulfilled it. Jesus lived a perfect life, and it is only by Jesus residing within us that we can also be found perfect. This is why Paul says in Galatians 2:20,

> I have been crucified with Christ. It is no longer I who live, but Christ who lives in me. And the life I now live in the flesh I live by faith in the Son of God, who loved me and gave himself for me.

We have been given an unfathomable gift. We understand that when someone gives a gift, we must accept that gift. It is no different here in that this isn't a gift that comes to us without our understanding or acceptance. We must accept this gift of God. Paul has already explained how we accept this gift in the 6th chapter. He says in verse 3, "Do you not know that all of us who have been baptized into Christ Jesus were baptized into his death?" We enter into Christ through baptism, and it is also at the point of baptism that we receive the Holy Spirit. (Acts 2:38) While baptism isn't mentioned in this section, it is instrumental to understanding the message Paul is trying to impart to the Romans.

In verses 5–8 of chapter 8, Paul expounds upon what he has said in verse 4. To live according to the flesh is to set your mind on the things of the flesh. To set the mind on the things of the flesh is to be hostile to God. This idea is thoroughly expounded upon in Galatians 5 where Paul talks about the work of the flesh. This is what Paul means when he talks about setting the mind on the things of the flesh. Yet, to set the mind on the spirit is life and peace. So, the comparison is between the flesh and the Spirit.

The answer Paul gives is incredibly simple. To be a Christian one must set his or her mind on the Spirit and not the flesh. Only one of these can please God, and it is not setting the mind on the flesh. What does Paul then say a Christian should do? Well, he says that "you" or rather, those who are in Christ are not in the flesh! Paul claims that if the Spirit of God dwells within Christians, then they belong to Christ. More than that, if Christ is found within Christians, then even though we ought to be dead in our sins, we are alive in Christ.

Consider the 11th verse:

If the Spirit of him who raised Jesus from the dead dwells in you, he who raised Christ Jesus from the

dead will also give life to your mortal bodies through
his Spirit who dwells in you.

We don't deserve what we have been given, in fact,
we deserve death and not life! Yet, God saw fit through
His Son to give us eternal life in Christ! We can know we
have this because of the Spirit that dwells within us. We
can know we have the Spirit because we receive it at the
point of baptism.

Application

How does this apply to us today? Well, if we are not in
Christ then we are condemned. Jesus condemned sin in
the flesh. Anyone who has ever sinned can be redeemed,
sanctified, and forgiven of their sins because sin has been
condemned. Jesus came to save people, not condemn
people. He has saved people by condemning sin! Thus,
the only way for us to be saved is by being in Christ. We
have received the helper (John 15:26), or the Spirit of
God as a confirmation of our salvation. The Spirit is what
continually cleanses us and keeps us holy and unblem-
ished. (1 John 1:7)

To keep things simple, we must be found in Christ if
we are to be saved. There is no alternative for salvation.
We must be focused on the things of the Spirit and not on
the things of the flesh. If we are focused on the things of
the flesh, it is impossible for us to please God. We must
submit to God, and we must be willing to live a life that is
pleasing to Him. Our aim today is the same as the
brethren in Rome, which is to live a life pleasing in God's

eyes. The possession of the Spirit of God is essential to living a life pleasing in God's eyes.

Conclusion

I have been asked many times how the Spirit works today. There is a distinct difference between the way the Spirit worked in the first century, and the way it works today. Certainly, the Spirit did then what it does now, but He also did more in the first century! So, what does the Spirit do now? The Spirit allows us to be found righteous in the eyes of God by continually cleansing our sin. The Spirit is a confirmation that we belong to God, that we are saved.

Discussion Questions

1. Can you be certain that you are saved?
2. If you can be certain, can you then explain the process by which you are saved?
3. What role does the Spirit play in your salvation?
4. How important is Jesus in the salvation of your soul?
5. What are the differences between living in the flesh vs. the Spirit?
6. Can you transition your body from dead to alive? If so, how?

Freedom Through Restoration
2 Corinthians 13
Scott Harp

READ 2 CORINTHIANS 13.

"Freedom!" resounded loudly from the lips of William Wallace, played by Mel Gibson, at the end of the 1995 movie classic Braveheart. The film depicted the revolt of the people of Scotland against the tyrannical rule of the English King Edward I "Longshanks" beginning in 1280 A.D. The dramatic cry resonated strongly with the film audience, but the scene's message was more critical. Willingness to die for freedom appeals to the core of all people.

The human experience thrives upon the right of one to direct his life steps. And yet, as old as time itself, as man has interacted with his neighbors, the struggle of carrying out his pursuits has been forcibly restrained. For societal freedom to exist, mutual understandings and even restrictions must be put in place by all involved. The trouble is that man's attempts at determining freedom for himself and his neighbors fail without God (Jer 10:23).

Freedom in Christ comes with no legal restraints if we pursue ". . . love, joy, peace, patience, kindness, goodness, faithfulness, gentleness, self-control . . ." (Gal 5:22–23). (All Scripture references from the English Standard Version unless otherwise noted). However, if pursuing freedom is selfish, and at the expense of those around us, including the Lord, it cannot be considered true freedom. A pilot can soar freely through the air but must submit to the instruments in the cockpit to take off and land safely. Similarly, the Scriptures are God's "instruments" on how all people of all ages can experience the highest sense of freedom. The root of ALL the errors charged against the church of Christ at Corinth was a selfish, "do it my way" mentality.

Gleaning from the first verse of the last chapter of three known Corinthians letters (2 Cor 13:1, 1 Cor 5:9), and two visits from Paul, with the intention of a third, we learn at least two things. First, the apostle loved this church like a parent would his little child. He established this congregation (Acts 18). These church members were his babes in Christ. The firmness in his voice resounds from the page as one of determinate counsel and persuasion. Second, referencing the Old Testament law of witness, "by the evidence of two or three witnesses" (Deut 17:6; 19:15), the apostle was letting the church know that his presence the third time would prove enough to indict and convict those who had not yet turned from their unfaithfulness (2 Cor 13:2).

Poor Paul! The man wore himself out for Jesus and poured himself out for His people (2 Cor 11:16–33). Yet, where was the respect? Where was the motivation to exercise true freedom through repentance and faithful living? One can just hear from the content of verses 2 and 3 the defiant tone of the naysayers, "Who died and made you the boss of me, Paul?" Yet, in weakness, this tried and tested warrior of faith exhibited the image of Christ's suffering in death and rise to power and strength in His resurrection. Paul's sacrifices and appointment as an apostle of Christ gave him the authority to demand faithfulness.

The last nine verses of the chapter potentially constitute the final words this congregation of the Lord's people would ever hear from heaven. The statements are short and arguably pithy. Yet together, they spell out the Holy Spirit's recipe for freedom in the Corinthian church and subsequently to all churches of Christ that should exist down through the ages.

The keys to freedom in Christ involve a look in the mirror. What do you see? Is the reflection a sure representation of what has been received in the gospel? When you initially obeyed, were you not changed? When you rose from that watery grave of baptism you received, ". . . the riches of the glory of this mystery, which is Christ in you, the hope of glory (Col 1:27). Look closely! In other words, "examine yourselves, to see whether you are in the faith. Test yourselves. Or, do you not realize this about yourselves, that Jesus Christ is in you?" (2 Cor 13:5). True Christians reflect Christ. Jesus lived a life of faithfulness, overcoming temptation, and stands as the most accurate example of one who always chose the right thing (Heb 4:15). Paul also stands as an example of faithfulness. In a previous letter, he said, "But I discipline my body and keep it under control, lest after preaching to others I myself should be disqualified" (1 Cor 9:27). Self-examination for the Christian is to let the Scriptures be the standard for transformation into the image of Christ.

Hear the urgency as the beloved apostle prayed for his Corinthian children in the faith. He knew the time of his departing this life could happen at any time. Significant changes had to take place to keep the work growing on the foundation of Jesus (1 Cor 3:11). The Holy Spirit's appeal was of utmost importance. Corinth had to do "what is right" (2 Cor 13:7), no matter what weakness they may have deemed apparent in their teacher. To help them, Paul shared these written words to clarify the proper and correct ways to live. For true freedom to exist, they had to make some choices.

Historically, disciplinary threats have had their place in bringing about good behavior (2 Cor 5:10–11). My mother's choice of corrective discipline was a small branch from a bush in our backyard. It was her practice not only to administer reprimand with it, but she often left the choice of weight and length to the recipient. Such responsibility is a study all its own. Timing was significant as well. Too much time taken to investigate which "weapon" of correction to select could lead to a firm warning from the back door, "Don't make me come down there!" Similarly, some dilly-dallying brethren heard, "For this reason, I write these things while I am away from you, that when I come, I may not have to be severe in my use of the authority that the Lord has given me for building up and not for tearing down" (2 Cor 13:10) In other words, "Corinth! Don't make me come down there!"

Restoration is the aim! The visits, the letters, the patience, the sacrifices, and the prayers were always about encouraging Christians to bring themselves back to the actual model of what Christ visualized for His people; to be like Him. In 2 Corinthians 13:9, Paul prayed for their *katartisis*, translated "perfection" in the King James Version, and rendered "restoration" in the English Standard Version. In verse 11, he used a different ending on the same word, kartartiso, "Be perfect" (KJV), or "Aim for restoration" (ESV). The clarion cry of God down through time, by way of His prophets, His preachers, His Son, the apostles, and the Scriptures, is for His people to make a choice for Him and for His way. Through restoration, true freedom could and can finally be achieved.

Gaze upon a restored antique vehicle. When one is seen, it immediately registers the labor-intensive effort that must have been involved in bringing it back to perfection. Most would look at an old rust bucket in the weeds and say, "It is impossible." But to a few, it would look like a challenge worth taking. Being at one with God, for most, looks impossible. But, to those who know their Father's love, it may be a long road home, but it is deemed a road worth traveling. Remember the Prodigal Son when he came to himself (Luke 15:17ff). When he began his trip home, no doubt he continued thinking of a new life of devoted servitude in his Father's house. For him, it was the only possible way to experience true freedom.

When restoration is the aim, mutual comfort and agreement among brethren follow. Why? Because it always has been, and always will be, that the God of love, through his Scriptures alone, can give us true peace and love. It has been the same for two millennia after the cross. The Reformers of the Middle Ages, and ultimately the voices of those in the American Restoration Movement, continued the cry of going back to the Scriptures for authority in all religious and spiritual matters. And, in so doing, true spiritual freedom can be achieved even to this day.

God is giving us time. Among the final words recorded from the apostle Peter are the following, "And count the patience of our Lord as salvation . . ." (2 Pet 3:15a). May "the grace of the Lord Jesus Christ and the love of God, and the fellowship of the Holy Spirit . . ." be with us, and grant to us all time and patience until we come to be fully reflective of all that is Jesus in our lives. Until then, spiritual liberty for all dictates that we must greet one another with proper acknowledgment of their place at our side, called "holy kisses" by the apostle (2 Cor 13:12–14); for it is only together in Christ that we will achieve and maintain true freedom.

The sentiments of 2 Corinthians 13 are vital to my life focus and discipline as a child of God. Restoration has been my life's challenge and mission. May we all heed the call of freedom in Christ as children of God.

Discussion Questions

1. Why is the concept of freedom so precious to so many people?
2. In what ways does the devil try to exploit our love for freedom?
3. How do we keep our freedom in Christ from degenerating into selfishness?
4. In what senses is the phrase "freedom through restoration" paradoxical?
5. Why is true freedom found only in Christ?
6. Why is restoration essential to finding true freedom?

www.TheRestorationMovement.com

Take Courage I Have Conquered the World

John 16:33

Don Snodgrass

I have said these things to you, that in me you may have peace. In the world you will have tribulation. But take heart; I have overcome the world (John 16:33)[1].

THESE ARE THE WORDS THE APOSTLE JOHN RECORDS as Jesus is making one more attempt to prepare His disciples for what will happen to Him during the next several hours. Before He prepares Himself for the upcoming events, Jesus takes time to try to prepare His disciples.

These words wrap up a very personal and emotional message to His disciples that began after Judas Iscariot left to betray Him (John 13:21–30) and concludes with the text cited above. A message that included the foretelling of Peter's denial, as well as the promise of the Holy Spirit. A message that foretold the disciples would soon experience great sorrow followed by great joy. In this last "sermon" before His crucifixion, Jesus tells them of His upcoming departure; that He will be going to prepare a place for them; that He will be reunited with them.

As we read John's record of Jesus's words in these four chapters, not only are we able to hear the words, but we can also sense the emotions and attitudes that accompany them. We sense Peter's overconfidence as he states his willingness to die for Jesus (13:37). We see a lack of full understanding by Thomas and Philip (14:1–11). And perhaps we even sense a bit of frustration from Jesus as He responds to His disciples during this conversation.

That in Me you may have peace. Jesus says that He has told these things to His disciples so they may have peace. But what kind of peace? Certainly not the kind of peace as the world understands the word. Afterall, in His next breath Jesus says we will have tribulations in this world. The immediate context (Jesus preparing His disciples for His death), would suggest that Jesus is referring to their respective state of mind. I think He is wanting them to understand that His death has been part of His mission from the beginning and there was nothing that they (or anyone else) could have done to stop it; "it's okay." But as we read the phrase more carefully, we see the phrase in me. Jesus is also talking about a peace that can only be found in Him. The Apostle Paul describes this as "the peace of God, which surpasses all understanding" (Phil 4:7). This peace is not the result of a well-funded retirement account or other worldly achievement. This is a peace with God through Jesus; a reconciliation between God and man.

It is vital we remember that each of us was an enemy of God, and that our reconciliation was made possible only by the sacrifice of Jesus (Rom 5:10). He brokered the peace between us and God. Many of us have seen the bumper stickers and T-shirts with the phrase, "Know Jesus, Know Peace. No Jesus, No Peace." I suspect the person who coined this phrase understood that the peace that comes from knowing Jesus requires more than a simple intellectual knowledge of Him. It requires knowing and following His teachings; being a disciple. The second part of the phrase is not only true for the individual on a personal level, but it also rings true on a larger scale. Without Jesus — without His sacrifice — there would be no peace, no reconciliation with God.

In the world you will have tribulation. Becoming a Christian does not guarantee an easy life. Being "in the world," we face what I would call "active" and "passive" tribulations. Passive tribulations are those we face despite our relationship with Jesus as we live in a world that has been contaminated by sin. Our relationship with Him does not make us immune to these. We continue to have financial struggles, personal difficulties, health problems, anxieties brought about by what we see in the world around us, and more. On the other hand, we experience "active" tribulations because of our relationship with Jesus.

Throughout His ministry, Jesus talked about the cost of being His follower. Just a few breaths earlier, He warned His disciples that there would be those who would "put you out of the synagogues" (16:1–4). From the martyrdom of Stephen (Acts 7), through the early years of the church, and even in our present-day, tribulations have been a component of following Jesus. As I write this chapter, several families come to my mind who are dealing with tribulations at this very moment. But Jesus did not end His message here.

But take heart. Jesus's message to His disciples did not end with Him telling them to get ready for tribulations. His message was — and is — one of hope. He called His disciples to "take heart," to "be of good cheer," and I would say take courage. Yes, He was trying to prepare them for the great sorrow that they would be experiencing soon. He was trying to let them know that it was going to look pretty dark. But He was also letting them know that they would not stay in this state of sorrow and darkness, and that following this brief period of darkness, their sorrow would become joy (16:16–24).

Sometimes that period of sorrow and darkness can seem very long; sometimes it may actually be very long. But Jesus has called us to "take heart" and remember His promise that ultimately — whether in this life or the next — our sorrow will be turned into joy. As we travel through these dark times, not only do we need to rely on Jesus, but we also need to turn to our brothers and sisters and lean on them. And as we see our brothers or sisters going through a dark time, we need to provide them with love, comfort, and support.

I have overcome the world. This is the reason Jesus was able to tell His disciples to take heart. Though it was going to appear that the world had defeated Jesus via the crucifixion, He assured His disciples that He had already overcome the world. This issue had already been decided and He was the victor.

From the historical accounts available to us, the

world in the first century was pretty violent, harsh, and bleak. The crucifixion itself tells us of the violence and harshness in the world at that time. For those without power, existence was hard, and the future was bleak. But Jesus overcame all of this and more to bring about a better world. Though sin and its consequences were still in the world, He left the world in a better condition than what it was when He came.

Jesus is stronger than anything we may have to face. Whatever the world may throw at us, Jesus has already overcome it and is with us to help us also overcome.

I chose to share this verse because of its message of reality and hope. Yes, we still live in an imperfect world that has been spoiled by sin resulting in the consequences that we all face. Whether we are dealing with what I have called the "passive" or "active" tribulations, this verse helps to remind us that we can allow ourselves to be at peace, knowing that Jesus will ultimately take care of us. This is not a "Pollyanna" attitude or a demonstration of naivety, as some in the world might say, but this is a faith in Jesus that has a proven track record. I am confident that most of you can look through your life events and can now see how Jesus brought you through these tribulations.

One of the things that I take away from this passage is that Jesus is in control. Too often, especially as a shepherd, I find myself thinking that it all depends on me. That's my ego leading me in the wrong direction. In more recent years, when I read the dialogue between Jesus and Thomas in chapter 14 of John, I sense frustration from Jesus when Thomas responds with, "Lord, we do not

know where you are going. How can we know the way?"
Jesus replies to him, "*I* am the way, ... " [emphasis mine]. I
try to carry that same emphasis on Jesus in our verse: "*I*
have overcome the world." Jesus has overcome the world,
not me. Jesus has control of the situation, not me. The
church depends on Jesus, not me. Do not get me wrong, I
have a responsibility in my role as a shepherd, but my
faith and my confidence are not to be in me, but always
in Him.

Discussion Questions

1. What gives you peace?
2. What types of "passive" and "active"
   tribulations do you face?
3. What reasons do you have to "be of good
   cheer?"
4. Do you think Jesus was ever frustrated with
   His disciples from time to time? What are
   some ways that we may frustrate Him today?
5. What evidence do you see today of Jesus
   overcoming the world?

Endnotes

[1] All scripture references are from the English Standard
Version unless stated otherwise.

Freedom in the Lord

2 Corinthians 3:17
Chris Keeton

Focus Passage

2 CORINTHIANS 3:17–18

> Now the Lord is the Spirit, and where the Spirit of
> the Lord is, there is freedom. And we all, with
> unveiled face, beholding the glory of the Lord, are
> being transformed into the same image from one
> degree of glory to another. For this comes from the
> Lord who is the Spirit.[1]

Introduction

You are what you look at. That's probably overstating my
case. Nevertheless, the media we consume and the stories
we pay attention to seem to have a significant effect on
how we live. For example, if we watch too much cable
news, then we might think that the most important thing
is who we vote for. Or, if our preferred social media plat-

form promotes one particular moral concern over any other, then we will probably be more interested in *that particular moral concern over any other*.

I'm not suggesting, of course, that we abandon contemporary media. Being aware of what is happening in the world is generally a good thing. I'm simply inviting us all to "pay attention to what we are paying attention to."[2] The very nature of the culture we live in is that its influence is everywhere. As most Christians are aware, culture can contain wicked influences. And culture is most nefarious when the cultural values sound religious.

We cannot escape our culture or our cultural influences, but we are not to be lead by those influences (Rom 12:2). As Christians, we desire to be Spirit led rather than culture led (Rom 8:1–8). The Corinthian church had trouble distinguishing between these two leadings. In our text, the apostle Paul graciously guides the church toward a more spiritual method of discernment. Part of that method is to simply ask—what are you looking at most of the time?

Going Deeper

Letters of Recommendation

Paul's running start into our focus passage begins with his mention of "letters of recommendation" in 3:1. Paul asks the Corinthians why he, and the rest of the apostolic ministers, need such letters. These kinds of letters were widely used in the ancient world to introduce friends and acquaintances to others. A person traveling to a new location may bring a letter of recommendation in order to establish credibility for the purpose of, for example, gaining employment.[3] Paul goes on to affirm that he doesn't need such a letter because they, the Corinthian church, already know him. This is not to say that Paul condemns recommendation letters in general. Paul himself recommends Phoebe at the end of his letter to the Romans (Rom 16:1–2). Moreover, Luke indicates that Apollos received letters of recommendation from fellow disciples.

The sticking point for Paul is that some of the Corinthians doubted Paul's credentials, which would then directly lead to doubting Paul's ministry in the Gospel. Paul is probably calling out these doubters in chapter 11 by calling them "false apostles" (11:13) and, sarcastically, "super-apostles" (11:5), because they thought far too highly of themselves. The whole project of these false apostles in Corinth was to build their own credibility through their appearance, accomplishments, intelligence, and skill (5:12, 10:10, 11:6). These values align so well with what we know about the culture of Corinth that we could say that these false apostles were preaching the "Gospel of Corinthian Success" instead of the Gospel of Jesus Christ.[4] Paul counters this cultural Gospel throughout 2 Corinthians by emphasizing the spiritual values of humility (10:1), suffering (4:7–12), faith (5:7), and spiritual sight rather than physical (4:16–18). Spiritual freedom also belongs on that list, and we will return to that idea shortly.

How to remove a veil

Paul contrasts the glory of the old covenant with the glory of the new in verses 12–16. When Moses received the old covenant, in the form of a written law code, his face shone in glorious brightness because he had been communing with God (Exod 34:29). Moses put a veil over his face to cover the brightness, but this wasn't what Moses, or God, intended. The shining face frightened the Israelites, and they would not go near him (Exod 34:30). The need for the veil arose because the minds of the Israelites were hardened (3:14). Paul, speaking symbolically, affirms that a veil remains over the minds of his unbelieving Jewish brothers. This symbolic veil represents a barrier between the people and God. This barrier could have been angry unbelief, like those who rejected Jesus at Nazareth (Luke 4:16–30), fear, like those Israelites who were afraid of God's glory shining off of Moses's face (Exod 34:30), or envy, like those chief priests who succeeded in killing Jesus (Mark 15:10).

Whatever particular barrier Paul has in mind, he tells us how it is removed—by turning to the Lord (3:16). When a person truly turns to the Lord, the veil drops away just as the scales dropped from Paul's own eyes in Acts 9:18. This state of unveiling and beholding the Lord without a barrier, just as Moses himself had done, belongs to those in the glorious new covenant.

The glory of the new covenant removes the necessity for physical artifacts driven by cultural pressures, like law codes (3:7) or letters of recommendation (3:1). David E. Garland sums up the issue nicely, "The law, when misinterpreted, seemed to encourage this do-it-yourself right-eousness and engendered this national pride that looked down on others."[5] This prideful religious outlook seemed to have been precisely what the "super-apostles" were preaching. Garland continues with the following regarding the unbelieving Israelites of Paul's day, but such could also be said of the prideful Corinthian Christians, and even some prideful Christians in our own day,

When we exalt ourselves, even for such a praiseworthy virtue as our zeal for God, we blind ourselves to God's exaltation. Those who are consumed with their own glory, with pride and boasting, will miss the glory of God revealed in Christ; for it is a peculiar sort of glory, one that radiates from the humiliation of the cross.[6]

Turning to the Lord in humility allows us to behold this "peculiar sort of glory." The result is spiritual freedom.

Where the Spirit of the Lord is, there is freedom

Arriving at our focus passage, Paul affirms that freedom and the Spirit of the Lord are in the same place. Paul seems to mean that his ministry to the Corinthians has been led by freedom. He has always been bold, open, and honest in his dealings with the Corinthians (2 Cor 7:8–12). He has felt uninhibited by cultural requirements, like letters of recommendation (2 Cor 3:1–3) or the demand by some to speak with flair (1 Cor 2:1–5, 2 Cor 1:12–14, 11:6). Paul was free to cast aside any superficial markers of prestige and was free to simply follow the Spirit and his love for the Corinthians (2 Cor 2:4, 5:14, 8:7, 11:11, 12:15). This freedom is available for the Corinthians, as well. They, like him, can also be free from superficial markers of prestige dictated by their culture.

And not only can they be like Paul, they can also be like Moses, who saw the glory of the Lord with an unveiled face. Paul explains that the turn to the Lord, first mentioned in v14, transforms the person as well as removes the veil. Seeing the glory of the Lord in this context probably means being open to the Spirit's action in their own lives and in the lives of their fellow believers. This, of course, would have been particularly relevant for the Corinthians because some were stuck looking at cultural markers for Paul's success and totally missed that they themselves were the markers of Paul's success (2 Cor 3:2). In other words, Paul's success could not be observed based on the authority of anyone who would write a letter of recommendation, rather, his success was observed by looking at each Spirit-filled believer in Corinth (2 Cor 3:3). Again, some Corinthians were restrained because they were looking at the wrong thing. Freedom comes when they look to the Lord.

Application

So, how do we know when we are being overly influenced by our culture? Finding an answer to that question is very difficult. And I know of no certain method that will guide us. However, perhaps a few simpler questions will get us started:

- What values do we hold tighter than others?
- What in the world makes us angry?
- What in the world gives us hope?
- What do we think about most of the time?
- What do we talk about most of the time?

If you answer these questions honestly and find that they line up perfectly with your favorite news host or social media influencer, then you've probably found the answer to our very difficult question.

Paul's invitation for each us is to turn to the Lord and behold his glory. We turn to the Lord when we retreat to pray, when we pay attention to God's constant presence within us, and when we pay attention each day to the Spirit's activity in our lives. We also behold God's glory when we see the Spirit's presence in our brothers and sisters in Christ. Each time we come to worship, take communion, and sing with our fellow disciples we are beholding God's transforming image in those very disciples.

The switch from being culture led to Spirit led may be as simple as changing what we look at most of the time.

Conclusion

The first sermon I preached for my church as their official preaching minister was on our focus passage. The years leading up to that point involved a few key changes for our church. And I knew that the coming months would contain more changes. Some changes were needed, others probably not. These changes were often preceded by asking questions such as, "What should we do now?" or "What will this person say if we don't?" or "Here's how other churches are doing this." These questions may be necessary, but such questions can also be vehicles for constraining cultural influences. God was calling us to ask a different kind of question before making decisions. One of those questions was, for example, "What feels most free?" Because, after all, where the Spirit of the Lord is there is freedom.

Discussion Questions

1. When you imagine God's glory, what do you see?
2. For those who are comfortable doing so, share a story about how God removed a veil or barrier in your life.
3. How might you differentiate cultural influences from spiritual influences in your daily life?
4. Considering that freedom and the Spirit are in the same place, what would you like to be free to do? What would you like to be free from?

Endnotes

[1] In this chapter we will use the ESV for all quotes from the Bible.

[2] I first came across this phrase in Curt Thompson's book *Anatomy of the Soul.* See Curt Thompson, *Anatomy of the Soul* (Carrollton, TX: Tyndale Momentum, 2010), 53.

[3] For further information see George H. Guthrie, 2 *Corinthians,* Baker Exegetical Commentary on the New Testament (Grand Rapids, MI: Baker Academic, 2015), 187.

[4] For further information on Corinthian culture see Guthrie 16.

[5] David E. Garland, 2 *Corinthians,* The Christian Standard Commentary (Brentwood, TN: B&H Publishing Group, 2021), 156.

[6] Garland, 156.

Did Philemon Reconcile?

Michael Farris

Focus Passage: Philemon

ONE OF THE MOST REFRESHING, REJUVENATING blessings shared between spiritual siblings is that of reconciliation.

One Main Thing / Introduction

Christ-like disciples practice the life-changing virtue of seeking and giving the forgiveness required for reconciliation. We have all been on both sides of offenses. We know the challenging emotions and thoughts when presented with the choice between bitterness and retribution, or love and reconciliation. As disciples of Christ, we must be like Onesimus; desiring to reconcile with our spiritual sibling. We must also be like Philemon, known for refreshing the hearts of the saints.

Going Deeper

Written concurrent with his epistle to the brethren in Colossae, Paul also wrote a brief, personal letter to a Christian named Philemon, a resident there. He wrote to *benefit* the process of reconciliation between Philemon and his runaway slave named Onesimus who is now Philemon's spiritual brother. The circumstances and subtleties within this account are better realized by a focus on slavery within the Roman Empire. Slaves were acquired through various means including *battle conquests, birth, or indebtedness.* Comprising nearly one-third of Rome's population, slaves were treated as living tools, void of a soul. Their *lives, treatment, and death* were at the discretion of their masters.

As for Onesimus, neither his pre-Christian attitude nor his work ethic benefited anyone. Under Roman law, if a runaway slave were to return, the master can punish as he sees fit. Common consequences were amputation, prison, or even death. At the very least, the letter for fugitive would be branded on their forehead.

Fleeing Colossae and traveling 1,200 miles to Rome, Onesimus likely had no initial intention of returning. But providentially, he encountered Paul. Their personal conversation is not recorded, but similar sentiments were likely spoken as written in Paul's epistle to the Ephesians. (Eph 6:5–9)

Regardless, Onesimus realized and accepted that his new Christ-centered life required the effort to make right his former wrongs against Philemon. Upon returning to face Philemon, he presented a very helpful letter from

Paul, a mutually cherished brother-in-Christ. Imagine Philemon's initial perplexity to see this thief and slave willingly return, having no clue of the letter's contents.

> Paul, a prisoner of Christ Jesus, and Timothy our brother, to Philemon our beloved friend and fellow laborer, to the beloved Apphia, Archippus our fellow soldier, and to the church in your house: Grace to you and peace from God our Father and the Lord Jesus Christ (Phlm 1–3 NKJV).

First, with a brief and pleasant greeting, Paul reminds Philemon of the blessing of their shared fellowship in Christ. Second, Paul spotlights the love that governs all Christian behavior. These are timely reminders.

> I thank my God, making mention of you always in my prayers, hearing of your love and faith which you have toward the Lord Jesus and toward all the saints, that the sharing of your faith may become effective by the acknowledgment of every good thing which is in you in Christ Jesus. For we have great joy and consolation in your love, because the hearts of the saints have been refreshed by you, brother. (Phlm 4–7).

Having spoken sincerely of Philemon's genuine faith and conduct, Paul knew these words would prepare his heart to consider the impending request. In verses 8–10, Paul conveys his looming request for Onesimus, who is now a "son in the faith" (Phlm 10), by appealing to the higher standard of Christ-like love. Paul and Philemon have tremendous respect for one another. Yet, Paul appeals for love to generate the right result.

Paul states that Onesimus is now mutually beneficial to the Lord's work (Phlm 11). Paul further describes a precious providential perspective to promote the full pardon (Phlm 15–16a). If Onesimus had not run, he may not have become a brother.

Paul continues. (Phlm 18) "But if he has wronged you or owes anything, put that on my account." Paul knows Roman law. He is exercising the clause of advocacy. In such a case, a close friend or partner could make a plea on the slave's behalf. This legal course allows for possible mercy. Paul's plea includes the offer to pay any debt if Philemon demands retribution. Although it is doubtful that Philemon would have pursued having Paul pay for Onesimus' offense, it certainly shows how confident Paul was of his conversion.

Notice how Paul pleads for reconciliation in verse 20. "Yes, brother, let me have *joy* from you in the Lord; refresh my heart in the Lord." The Greek word often translated as joy is rendered *benefit* in the NIV. Paul wants the *benefit* of *refreshment* that Philemon is accustomed to giving.

This key Greek word is 'Onimin,' the root word of the name Onesimus. Paul is essentially saying, *"Philemon, I know he wasn't much 'joy/benefit' to you, but I want some 'joy/benefit' from you.' Would you give me some Onimen by your complete forgiveness of Onesimus?"* (Phlm 17)

Paul wants Philemon to welcome Onesimus back not merely as the slave he was but now as the brother he is.

Philemon is faced with a decision. He could exercise his rights under Roman Law. He could do what is right under Christ's higher law. Which will it be? The inspired text gives no follow-up. Perhaps, it does not need to.

Application

Paul knew this personal matter between Philemon and Onesimus was not his to handle. Yet, we learn much from his inspired approach to assist. Christ-centered reconciliation requires ...

1. being prayerful (Phlm 4–6). Notice Paul's emphasis on faith, love, giving, and understanding of every blessing in Christ. Colossians 1:19–23 teaches how reconciliation is both a process and a power completely enabled by God! This is why the whole process must be immersed in prayer.

2. being polite (Phlm 8–9). Pride and arrogance always sabotage relationships. Paul knew better than to boss Philemon in this personal matter. Paul emphasizes love to encourage the right decision.

3. preserving privacy (Phlm 10,14). For the cause of Christ, do not broadcast offenses. Gossip acts like spiritual cancer and will only harm the Lord's Body.

4. being personal. Paul was helpful but knew his boundaries. This matter was truly to be

> resolved first between the two (Matt 18:15–35).
>
> 5. possessing the spirit of partnership (Phlm 17). The mindset of the body—membership (1 Cor 12:12–13:8) asserts that Onesimus is now just as much a member of the Lord's body as Paul and Philemon. When offense threatens fellowship, love compels every effort to restore it (Eph 4:31–32; Matt 6:12; 18:21–35).

God's redeemed saints must mature in the spiritual discipline of reconciliation. Pursuing and practicing God's will in this matter assures His presence and providence for the benefit (cf. Mtt. 18:15–35).

Having responded in faith to the gospel's call, the Lord forgave Onesimus (Acts 2:38; Rom 6:3–6). Will Philemon now manifest the spirit of Christ and do what he knows will refresh the heart of both Paul and Onesimus? (Eph 4:32)

Conclusion

Philemon is a short epistle, but it would be difficult to find another story as beautiful as this one. Jesus's disciples must nurture a heart of genuine devotion to Him and love toward the brethren. This facilitates the forgiveness we often must seek and be naturally inclined to offer. The Lord's will is not always easy, but the rejuvenating blessings of reconciliation are eternally refreshing.

Resources

Extra-biblical sources can often provide interesting historical insights. Fifty years after Paul's letter concerning Onesimus, (nearly twenty years after all New Testament was completed), a first-century Christian writer named Ignatius, would be martyred in Rome.

During the journey, he stopped in Smyrna and wrote encouraging letters to a few congregations. In his letter to Christians in Ephesus, he wrote, "...to the wonderful minister and Elder, Onesimus." Is this more than a mere coincidence? Many argue this is the same person mentioned in Paul's letter to Philemon. If so, Ignatius shows us that a "formerly useless [slave] has become useful to all"? (Phlm 11)

Please use this URL to read from Ignatius' letter to the Ephesians. https://www.biblestudytools.com/history/early-church-fathers/ante-nicene/vol-1-apostolic-with-justin-martyr-irenaeus/ignatius/

Please use this URL to further study slavery in the New Testament world. https://www.psephizo.com/biblical-studies/what-was-slavery-like-in-the-nt-world/

Discussion Questions

1. How does conversion affect one's work ethic?
2. How do you suppose this matter was discussed between Paul & Onesimus?
3. How do you suppose Onesimus felt while traveling back to Philemon?

4. How do you suppose Philemon felt just after reading Paul's letter?
5. Would there have been any justifiable reason for Philemon not forgive? Why?
6. The Big Question: What was Philemon's decision?

Scripture Index

Scripture Index

Scripture Index

Credits

Contributors

Mike Baker — BA (2001) is the Pulpit Minister for the Green Hill Church of Christ in Mount Juliet, Tennessee.

Chris Carrillo — MMin (2022) Education and Outreach Minister for Keller Church of Christ in Keller, Texas.

Bryan Collins —BA (2000) and MA (2004) is Associate Professor and Director of the Faulkner University Campus in Huntsville, AL. He preaches for the Mimosa Church of Christ in Fayetteville, Tennessee.

Robert Darby — AA (1998) and BA (1999) is retired from innercity ministry work.

Michael Farris — AA (2003) and BA (2010) is Pulpit Minister for Oak Hill Church of Christ in Rome, Georgia oak-hill.org.

Jordan Gray — MMin (2016) preaches for the Central congregation in Fayette, Alabama (facebook.com/central-cofcfayette). He and his wife, Priscilla, also walk with couples and speak with churches concerning marriage crisis, glorifying God for the story of redemption He worked out in their own marriage.

Scott Harp — BA (1989) was selected Alumnus of the Year in 2021. He is the minister for the Crittenden Drive church of Christ in Russellville, Kentucky, and editor for TheRestorationMovement.com

George Hulett —BA (1998) preaches for the Downtown Church of Christ in Morrilton, Arkansas since 2011.

Chris Keeton — BA (2005) DMin (2020) serves as the preaching minister for the Hernando Church of Christ in Hernando, Mississippi. He previously served as the youth minister for ten years. Chris and his wife, Cassidy, have three children, Ben (5), Matthew (2), and Embree (1).

Jerry Self — BA (1980) serves on the Board of Directors of Heritage Christian University. He serves as an elder with the Winfield Church of Christ in Winfield, Alabama.

Don Snodgrass — MA (2016) serves as a shepherd for the Sherrod Avenue church of Christ in Florence, Alabama. He and his wife, Rosemary, are retired and are involved with mission efforts including teaching in the Philippines and South Africa, as well as conducting workshops/seminars for different congregations.

Onesimus Bible Study Series

The Onesimus Bible Study Series offers biblical lessons for personal or group study from alumni of International Bible College/Heritage Christian University. Each lesson flows from confidence in Scripture as God's inspired, living, and powerful word. Each respects the ongoing relevance of the Bible as it shows us God's heart and guides our service in the name of Jesus. Every lesson is designed to build faith and encourage Christian living.

Love of the Faith: Favorite New Testament Texts (2023)

Refreshing the Saints: Favorite Old Testament Texts (2024)

Confident of Your Obedience: Favorite Sermon on the Mount Passages (2025)

Joy and Comfort: Favorite Psalms (2026)

Also by Cypress Publications: Berean Study Series

To see full catalog of Heritage Christian University Press
and its imprint Cypress Publications, visit
www.hcu.edu/publications

www.ingramcontent.com/pod-product-compliance
Lightning Source LLC
Chambersburg PA
CBHW021653120626
46545CB00002B/847